Dealing With

WHEN
PEOPLE DIE

by Jane Lacey

Illustrated by Venitia Dean

W

Ess

D1099695

301 5021742409 5

Franklin Watts
Published in paperback in Great Britain in 2019 by The Watts Publishing
Group

Copyright © The Watts Publishing Group, 2017

All rights reserved.

Credits
Series Editor: Sarah Peutrill
Series Design: Collaborate

Every attempt has been made to clear copyright. Should there be any
inadvertent omission please apply to the publisher for rectification.

ISBN 978 1 4451 5798 6

Printed in China

Franklin Watts
An imprint of
Hachette Children's Group
Part of The Watts Publishing Group
Carmelite House
50 Victoria Embankment
London EC4Y 0DZ

An Hachette UK Company
www.hachette.co.uk

www.franklinwatts.co.uk

FSC
www.fsc.org

MIX
Paper from
responsible sources
FSC® C104740

Contents

I DON'T KNOW WHAT'S HAPPENING!

Lola's granny has died but her family haven't told her yet. They stop talking when she comes into the room. Lola feels worried and afraid. She doesn't know what is going on but she knows it is something bad.

Ewan is Lola's big brother

Lola keeps asking me, "Where's Granny? What's happened?" I want to tell her but Mum and Dad say Lola's too young to understand about Granny dying. But not knowing is making Lola feel unhappy.

Granny was staying with us because she was ill. Mum was looking after her. One evening, there was lots of running about, whispering and phone calls. No one would tell me what was happening. Mum asked me to stay in my bedroom.

I saw an ambulance from my bedroom window. They took Granny away. Mum says Granny isn't coming back, but she won't tell me why. What's happened to Granny? Are they whispering because they don't want me to know that Granny doesn't love us any more?

5

What can Lola do?

Lola is worrying because she doesn't know what's happened to her granny. She can:

★ tell her mum she is worried
★ ask why Granny has gone away
★ say not knowing is making her think frightening things.

What Lola did

I told Mum I thought Granny wasn't coming back because she didn't love us. So Mum gave me a hug and told me Granny had died. I burst into tears because I'll never see Granny again. Mum said Granny loved us and her love will never leave us.

I feel a bit better but I wish Granny was still here.

WHAT IS DEATH?

Death is when someone's body stops working and can't be made better.

Death is a natural part of life. All living things - plants, animals and people - grow older and eventually die one day. Living things don't live forever.

People die because their body gets old and worn out. They die because they are too ill to get better. Sometimes people die because they have a very bad accident.

A dead body can't feel pain or know what's going on.

I DON'T WANT TO SAY GOODBYE!

Tim finds it hard to believe his dad has died. He won't go to the funeral to say goodbye because he wants to think he will see his dad again.

George

Tim

George is Tim's friend

I know Tim's dad has died, but he keeps talking about him as if he is still alive. He got really cross with me when I said I was sorry about his dad.

Tim's story

Dad hasn't been well for ages. He's had medicine and operations and they've always made him feel better! But Mum says that Dad got too ill for the medicine to work any more. She says Dad died.

I can't believe Dad died. I think, if I don't say goodbye to Dad and if I don't go to the funeral, he'll walk in the door again, smiling! I'm afraid if I say goodbye I really will never see him again.

9

It would help Tim to accept that he won't see his dad again. He can:

* talk to his mum about it and listen to what she says
* go to his dad's funeral and say goodbye
* write a goodbye letter

What Tim did

I told Mum I didn't want Dad to be dead. We both cried together. Mum said I could write Dad a letter. She said people who loved Dad would be at his funeral. We would all remember him and say goodbye. I'm going to the funeral. It helps to think I won't be the only one saying goodbye.

WHAT HAPPENS AT A FUNERAL?

At a funeral, the person who has died is put in a wooden box called a coffin. Their body is either buried, which means put in the ground, or it is cremated, which means burned. Their name is written on a gravestone, a plaque or in a special book of remembrance.

Family and friends of the person who has died get together to remember them and say goodbye.

A religious service or ceremony may be held.

11

I'M ANGRY WITH MY BROTHER FOR LEAVING ME

Wes's older brother Henry died in an accident. Wes feels angry with his brother for leaving him on his own and making his mum and dad unhappy.

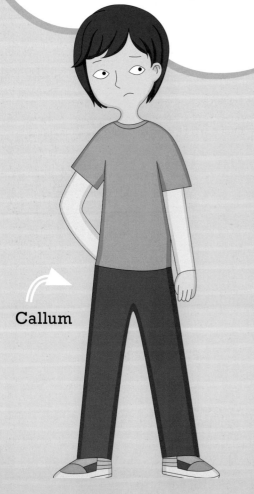

Callum

Callum is Wes's friend

Since Henry died, Wes is angry all the time - with Henry for dying and with his mum and dad about everything! He gets really angry if I talk about my big brother. I can't say anything right!

Wes's Story

A car knocked my big brother Henry off his bike and hurt him so badly he died.

I'm angry with Henry. I keep thinking he should have been more careful!

Now Mum and Dad are sad all the time. I can't talk about Henry because it makes them even sadder.

And they worry about me. They keep saying, "Be careful, Wes!" They won't let me ride my bike any more.

My friend Callum's big brother is alive but mine is dead. It's not fair!

Wes

Wes's mum and dad feel sad and worried because of Henry's accident. Wes can talk to a grown-up he trusts. He can:

★ say he feels angry with Henry
★ say he knows his mum and dad worry about him
★ say he doesn't like it when they think he is going to have an accident, too.

what wes did

I talked to Uncle Pete and he talked to Mum and Dad. Now they let me ride my bike in the park. I'm taking a cycling test so I will know how to stay safe when I ride on the road. I think Mum and Dad will always worry about me more because of what happened to Henry.

14

WILL I EVER STOP FEELING SAD?

Emily's mum died a year ago but Emily often feels sad. She wonders if she will ever be happy again.

Molly

Emily

Molly is Emily's friend

Sometimes when Emily and I are having fun and she's laughing and happy, she suddenly gets sad and won't play any more. I know she's thinking about her mum but she won't talk about it.

Emily's Story

On Wednesday it's the anniversary of Mum's death. It's a whole year since she died, but I still feel sad.

Every time I do something I used to do with Mum, I miss her and feel like crying because she isn't here any more. I cried when Dad helped me make my birthday cake because Mum and I always did it together. Dad cried, too.

Sometimes I forget that Mum has died and I feel happy. Then I remember and I feel sad again.

what can Emily do?

Emily will always miss her mum. It helps to have happy memories. She can:

★ tell her friend Molly how she feels
★ talk to her dad
★ plan to do something on the anniversary of her mum's death so that it isn't just a sad day.

what Emily did

I talked to Dad and he said he still feels sad, too. We decided to make Wednesday a special day for Mum. We cooked her favourite meal, went on her favourite walk and even told her favourite jokes! We'll always be sad that Mum died, but we don't always have to be sad when we remember her.

17

I'M AFRAID I WILL DIE TOO

Luke thought that only pets and very old people died. So when his friend Max died he was shocked. Now Luke is afraid of dying, too.

Jack is Luke's friend

Jack

Luke and Max were my best friends. Max died because he was very ill. Now Luke thinks he's going to die, too. But just because Max died, it doesn't mean Luke or I are going to die.

Luke

Luke's Story

I was sad when my pet hamster died and I cried when Nan died. But I didn't worry because hamsters don't live for very long and Nan was very old.

Then Max died. He was only a kid like me! Now I think about dying all the time. I worry that Mum and Dad will die. I worry that I will die. I can't get to sleep. When I do, I have nightmares. I go into Mum and Dad's room to make sure they are okay.

Jack keeps saying, "Of course you won't die!" He gets fed up with me. I don't want to tell Mum and Dad in case they get fed up with me, too. I wish I didn't feel so afraid.

19

what can Luke do?

Worrying about dying is making Luke unhappy. He can:

★ tell his mum and dad he is afraid of dying
★ say he is afraid they will die.

what Luke did

I told Mum and Dad. They said everyone has to die at some point, but there was no reason to think any of us would die soon. They said I must tell them when I feel afraid. But I don't feel so afraid now I've talked to them. I do miss Max though.

MY PARENTS DON'T LOVE ME ANY MORE

Sophia's mum and dad are sad that baby Layla died. Sophia thinks they loved baby Layla more than they love her.

Sophia

Priti

Priti is Sophia's friend

Sophia told me her mum and dad talk about Layla all the time. She thinks they wish she had died and not Layla. She tries to be good so they will love her more. But I said, "Our mums and dads love us when we're good and when we're bad."

Sophia's Story

Layla died when she was only a baby. Mum and Dad talk about how sweet and good she was. They say, "Layla would have been a lovely girl."

I'm not sweet and good all the time. Sometimes I'm naughty. So I think Mum and Dad wish Layla was alive instead of me.

I try to be good so they'll love me and be glad I didn't die. Sometimes, I feel angry with Layla. I feel bad about that.

what can Sophia do?

★ remember - her mum and dad love her and they
would be very sad if she died
★ tell her mum and dad how she feels.

what Sophia did

I told Mum and Dad I thought they wished it was me and not Layla who had died. I said I would try to be good. They gave me a big hug and said they loved me all the time - even when I was naughty. They don't wish Layla was alive instead of me. Now I know they love me, I'm not angry with Layla any more.

I MISS GRANDAD, TOO

Jayden thinks no one knows how much he misses his grandad. Jayden's grandad was very popular with his family, as well as his friends. They are all sad he died but Jayden is very sad, too.

Ali

Ali is Jayden's friend

I know Jayden really misses his grandad. His mum, dad, aunts and uncles all help each other when they feel sad. I try to help Jayden when he feels sad.

Jayden

Jayden's Story

Grandad was my dad's father. Everyone loved him. He had lots of stories to tell and he was kind and funny. He called me his "little pal" and we did things together.

When he died, everyone was sad - Dad, Mum, my uncles and aunts and Grandad's friends. When they get together to remember Grandad, I feel left out.

I miss Grandad just as much as they do.

I'm afraid if I talk to Dad or Mum about Grandad, it will make them sad all over again.

What can Jayden do?

He can:

* talk to his friend Ali
* talk to his mum and dad or his aunts or uncles
* tell them he misses his grandad and that he feels left out.

What Jayden did

I talked to Ali. He said the grown-ups would understand that I missed Grandad too. So I talked to Grandad's sister. She is making a book with photographs and letters and stories about Grandad, and I'm helping her. We put something new in the book when we feel sad about Grandad and it helps us feel a bit better.

HOW CAN I REMEMBER SOMEONE SPECIAL?

Someone who has died can always be part of you. Remember:

★ special things they did and said
★ happy times together
★ games and jokes you shared
★ books and television programmes you both enjoyed.

You could also:

★ make a photo album
★ make a box of memories. Put in things such as a card they sent to you, a scarf they wore or their favourite poem
★ help to raise money for charity in their memory
★ plant a tree for them and watch it grow.

WHEN OUR FRIEND DIED

When Caitlin and Logan's friend Ruby died, they were shocked and very sad.

Caitlin and Logan's Story

Caitlin:

When our dog Sandy died, I was really sad that I wouldn't see him again. I never thought the same could happen to one of my friends.

Logan:

When Ruby died, I was really shocked. I thought only old people died.

Caitlin:

Logan and I were Ruby's best friends. Ruby's mum and dad asked if we wanted to go to Ruby's funeral. I wasn't sure. I'd never been to a funeral.

Logan:

Caitlin asked me if I wanted to go. I wasn't sure either, but I'm really glad we went.

Caitlin: At Ruby's funeral, her mum and dad, her big brother and our teacher all talked about Ruby and how special she was.

Logan: All the children in our class wrote something for Ruby. There were letters, poems, stories and even jokes.

Caitlin: Her mum and dad read some of them aloud at the funeral. Then they put them with the flowers and cards people had sent.

Logan: Ruby's mum and dad said they were very pleased we had come to the funeral.

Caitlin: I felt really sad when I got home and I cried. Mum gave me a hug and said I would begin to feel better but it might take a long time.

Logan: At school, we planted a tree for Ruby. I think about her every time I see it.

Caitlin: Now we don't feel sad about Ruby all the time. We are often happy and have fun but it doesn't mean that we have forgotten Ruby.

GLOSSARY

Accident
Something that happens suddenly and unexpectedly. Some very bad accidents can hurt or even kill people.

Afraid
You are afraid when you feel worried about something bad happening.

Alive
People, plants and animals are all alive. When you are alive you move, eat, sleep, learn and grow.

Ambulance
A van with special equipment that carries people to and from hospital.

Anniversary
An anniversary is when you remember something that happened on the same date every year. Your birthday is the anniversary of the day you were born.

Die
When someone dies, they are not alive any more.

Funeral
A funeral takes place when somebody dies and their body is buried or cremated.

Miss
You miss someone when you feel sad that you don't see them any more.

Sad
You are sad when you feel unhappy. When you feel sad you sometimes want to cry.

Worry
You worry when you don't know what is going to happen and you think something bad might happen.

Further information

For children

kidshealth.org/en/kids/somedie.html
Learn about what happens when someone dies and how to deal with your feelings.

childbereavementuk.org/young-people
If someone close to you has died, or are very ill, you can call or email Child Bereavement UK.

www.childline.org.uk
Tel: 0800 1111
Childline is a free helpline for children in the UK. You can talk to someone about any problem and they will help you to sort it out.

For parents

www.winstonswish.org/
Help for grieving children and their families.

www.cruse.org.uk
Cruse promotes the wellbeing of bereaved people and to enable anyone bereaved by death, including children, to understand their grief and cope with loss.

www.familylives.org.uk
Helpline for parents:
0808 800 2222
Family Lives offers advice and support for parents who are concerned about their children

For readers in Australia and New Zealand

kidshelpline.com.au
Tel: 1800 55 1800
Kidshelp is the free helpline for children in Australia. You can talk to someone about any problem.

www.kidsline.org.nz
A helpline run by specially trained young volunteers to help kids and teens deal with troubling issues and problems.

Note to parents and teachers: Every effort has been made by the Publishers to ensure these websites are suitable for children, that they are of the highest educational value and that they contain no inappropriate or offensive material. However, because of the nature of the Internet, it is impossible to guarantee that the contents of these sites will not be altered. We strongly advise that Internet access is supervised by a responsible adult.

INDEX

Notes for parents, carers and teachers

Children can feel sad and confused when someone they love dies. They often don't really understand what has happened. There are many ways that adults can help children deal with their grief.

- Children need to know what has happened and understand that the person who has died will not come back.
- Being able to express thoughts and feelings is an important part of dealing with grief.
- Questions, doubts and fears should always be taken seriously.
- It helps children to share happy memories of the person who has died.

Page 5 Lola's story

Lola's parents think she is too young to be told her granny has died. She thinks Granny has gone away because she doesn't love her any more.

- Children need to be told plainly what has happened – that Granny has died – not that she is asleep or has gone away.

Page 9 Tim's story

Tim doesn't want to go to his dad's funeral. He won't face the fact he'll never see his dad again.

- A funeral gives children a chance to share grief and happy memories with other people. Saying goodbye can help them to accept what has happened.

Page 13 Wes's story

When Wes's big brother was killed in a road accident, Wes was angry with his parents for worrying about him.

- It helps parents to remember that their grief over the death of a child can affect how they act towards their other children.

Page 16 Emily's story

Emily is worried she will never stop feeling sad about her mother's death.

- An anniversary of someone's death can be turned into an opportunity to share happy memories of them.

Page 19 Luke's story

Ever since his friend died, Luke has been worried about dying.

- Children need to know that everyone dies eventually. Understanding that early death is unlikely can help them to overcome fears and get on with normal life.

Page 22 Sophia's story

Sophia is unhappy because she thinks her parents wish she had died, not her baby sister.

- Children need to know that they are special and that their parents love them for who they are.

Page 25 Jayden's story

Jayden doesn't want to upset his parents by telling them how much he misses his grandad.

- Another member of the family or a friend can sometimes help a child with their grief if the parents are too sad themselves.

Page 28 Playscript: Caitlin and Logan's story

Children could 'perform' the parts in this simple playscript and then discuss what happened.